I0441933

Psychology

Hypnosis & Mind Control to Overcome Stress, Anxiety, Depression & Finally Recover Your Happiness

Fred McGuaghy

Fred McGuaghy

© **Copyright 2015 - All rights reserved.**

In no way is it legal to reproduce, duplicate, or transmit any part of this document in either electronic means or in printed format. Recording of this publication is strictly prohibited and any storage of this document is not allowed unless with written permission from the publisher. All rights reserved.

The information provided herein is stated to be truthful and consistent, in that any liability, in terms of inattention or otherwise, by any usage or abuse of any policies, processes, or directions contained within is the solitary and utter responsibility of the recipient reader. Under no circumstances will any legal responsibility or blame be held against the publisher for any reparation, damages, or monetary loss due to the information herein, either directly or indirectly.

Respective authors own all copyrights not held by the publisher.

Legal Notice:

This book is copyright protected. This is only for personal use. You cannot amend, distribute, sell, use, quote or paraphrase any part or the content within this book without the consent of the author or copyright owner. Legal action will be pursued if this is breached.

Disclaimer Notice:

Please note the information contained within this document is for educational and entertainment purposes only. Every attempt has been made to provide accurate, up to date and reliable complete information. No warranties of any kind are expressed or implied. Readers acknowledge that the author is not engaging in the rendering of legal, financial, medical or professional advice.

By reading this document, the reader agrees that under no circumstances are we responsible for any losses, direct or indirect, which are incurred as a result of the use of information contained within this document, including, but not limited to, —errors, omissions, or inaccuracies.

Table of Contents

Introduction 7

Chapter 1 - Hypnosis and Mind Control 11

Chapter 2 – Hypnotherapy for Anxiety, Depression and
Stress 15

Chapter 3 - Repressed Memory... 53

Chapter 4 – Cognitive Behavior Therapy.......................... 63

Chapter 5 – The Power of Biofeedback............................. 77

Chapter 6 – Manipulating Your Biofeedback 81

Chapter 7 – Creating Pain Levels 85

Chapter 8 – Manipulating Self Esteem Levels.................. 93

Chapter 9 – Mind Control Over Anger.............................. 97

Chapter 10 – Applying Therapeutic Psychology to Your
Life... 103

Conclusion.. 109

Fred McGuaghy

Introduction

There are times in life when you feel that things are escalating out of control. You are required to get through a certain amount of work, for example, or you may be asked to do things that you are uncomfortable with. The problems facing people in the world today are vast but can you imagine being totally in control of how you respond to all of the changes that happen within a lifetime? It's very powerful stuff, and mind control is not about cult behavior although it can be. In this case, we are talking about YOU being in control of your own mind and body and being able to glean so much from life because of that control.

Did you know that the way that you react to different stimuli depends upon your previous experiences or phobias and these can be helped with such treatments as hypnosis? Did you know that your conditioning as a human being starts when you are a child and continues throughout your life? There are indeed a diverse range of Therapeutic Psychology & Manipulation Techniques which are used these days to help people to better understand themselves and to make the most of their lives. You may just need to understand a little more about how these can help you before you take the reins of your life and use Therapeutic Psychology & Manipulation Techniques to help you to live the most fulfilling life that you can.

This book is your introduction to techniques that are used to help you and some of these require you to work on your own at home, as well as in a therapeutic situation with professionals because, at the end of the day, the ultimate responsibility for your well being rests with you. However, specialist help can get you on the right track. This book gives an overview of all the different treatments that are used to make the patient feel differently about the problems that everyday life keeps on presenting. Once you employ any of these kinds of treatments, you can go forward in your life with more confidence, better able to understand what is happening to you and why and able to control your mind. The book was written because I feel that too many people are put into dilemmas that they don't know how to face. Would you know how to give up an addiction if your life depended upon it? Would you know how to face something that is forced upon you by life even though you have a deep-rooted phobia?

What about problems that are housed in your subconscious that affect your beliefs in life? Can you deal with these when they eventually surface or will they break you into small pieces? Often in a psychologist's office, the paper tissues mop up the tears of those who have never learned to let out their emotions and have kept them bottled inside. The human brain is complex and when you put the complexity of life together with forcing a human being to make difficult and sometimes threatening decisions, it's too much for them.

There is help available and reading this book will help you to understand the types of manipulative therapies that may be applicable in your case and see how they work to help people to overcome problems. By reading it and understanding these techniques, you give yourself a head start in understanding what can be done to make your life an easier place to live in and move forward from your treatment in a way that's much more rewarding simply because you faced your demons and managed to come out of the other side of events within your life as a stronger and more capable human being.

Some of the suggestions involve professional help, while other chapters deal with things that you can do to manipulate the way that you think so that the outcome is much more positive and you get to benefit from it in the best way possible. The book had been written in an attempt to help people to see how much power they have over the course their lives take. I am in the driving seat of my life. Are you?

Chapter 1
Hypnosis and Mind Control

You may not have any experience of what hypnosis is all about and how it helps you to control the way in which your mind thinks. It's a very effective treatment for many things and this chapter tells you how it works. There are a small percentage of people that cannot be hypnotized but the majority can. Stanford University School of Medicine found out that there are reasons why some people cannot use this kind of treatment effectively. Using modern technology and imaging processes, they found that certain people have less activity in what they call the "executive function" part of the brain and little cohesion between the activity in this part of the brain and other parts. That is of course simplifying the whole question though basically, it means that 25 percent of patients from the practice of the researcher really do not respond to hypnosis while the 75 percent left do. What's interesting is that the MRI techniques used to decipher the difference in brain activity gives a very clear indication of why this is happening, so there may be hope for those who are unable at present to be hypnotized when systems are developed in the future that can allow for the difference in brain activity.

For the time being, a client typically goes to a hypnotist when they have a problem that they think that the hypnotist can help them with. These would typically be:

- Speech impediments

- Giving up smoking

- Alcoholism

- Phobias

- Weight Control

- Chronic pain control

- Memory and age related regression

- Concentration levels

- Regressive therapy

Typically a patient is asked to relax and will be sitting in a comfortable patient chair during the whole process. Sometimes, they will be given a headset to listen to the words of the therapist and will be asked to close their eyes to cut out distraction. The voice of the therapist is usually calming and comforting and the words that are used during the treatment will depend upon what the patient is being treated for. For example, for a smoke cessation session, the initial treatment would be to relax the patient so that they are in a "trance" state and are more susceptible to suggestion. This suggestion may take several forms but the overall intention of the therapy is to make the patient feel bad when they think about smoking a cigarette in the future. Some therapists offer up to six sessions for stopping smoking but it really depends upon how susceptible the patient is to the treatment.

One patient recounted to me how she felt that her treatment was unsuccessful because of several reasons and they may just have been valid reasons:

- The guy hypnotizing her had a lisp which stopped her from concentrating on the words

- She could clearly hear the traffic outside the therapy office and this distracted her

Thus one needs to find a therapist with a good success rate and also a voice that doesn't set your teeth on edge!

In all sessions of hypnotherapy, the patient is made comfortable and is taken into the trance state, which is where they are extremely relaxed and less inhibited about the way that they respond to instructions. In 1992, a study by the University of Iowa claimed that hypnotherapy was the most successful method of quitting smoking and this was confirmed in 2001 when a success rate as impressive of 90.26 percent was declared after a study on more than 6000 patients. That must make a pretty persuasive argument in favor of the use of hypnosis for cessation purposes such as for cigarette smoking and drug and alcohol use.

Chapter 2

Hypnotherapy for Anxiety, Depression and Stress

There are many people amongst us who suffer from several problems including stress, anxiety and depression. These problems can cause a normally functioning person to become extremely dependent or even unwilling to live. To get themselves out of such conditions, people will try almost anything. One therapy that stands out is hypnotism. While a lot of doctors claim that hypnosis and specially, self-hypnosis is not a real treatment, they cannot deny the fact that it seems to help a large number of people. In this chapter we will focus on how hypnosis and self-hypnosis can be used to elevate feelings of anxiety, stress and depression.

What Is Hypnosis?

Hypnosis is a state of mind where the body is in a trance. This state of mind allows you to maintain a period of extreme concentration and focus. Hypnotism ensures that a calm and relaxed manner prevails over you, which is why it is so popular amongst people who are stressed or suffer from anxiety attacks. Hypnosis allows you to enter a state of mind where you can take back the control over your mind and make it relax.

What Is Self-Hypnosis?

Self-hypnosis is the act of putting yourself under hypnosis and is generally considered more difficult to perform than hypnosis. In principle it is don't by trying to change the faith and mental associations that make you think, feel and act the way you do. Since most mental illnesses revolve around a person's negative influences or feelings in a situation, self-hypnotism is a useful tool in controlling these negative feelings and channeling them into a more positive direction.

How hypnosis and self-hypnosis work

Everything you feel, speak, think and act gets registered and stored in your brain. This includes your fears and negative thoughts. How you feel or what you think of a situation or place or thing greatly affects your reaction and behavior associated with that situation or place or thing. So, if you can change those feelings and thoughts your behavior will change accordingly.

Hypnosis and self-hypnosis use verbal persuasion to alter these negative thoughts in an attempt to allow you to regain control of your life. For example, supposing you have an irrational fear of water. Using hypnosis, you could possibly coax your brain not to associate the feeling of fear with water. Just by using your words you can make the change in your behavior. However, this isn't as easy as it sounds. It takes a lot of time and patience to rewire your brain into thinking the way you want it to. Amygdala are twin clusters of neurons in your brain that play a major role in this rewiring process as they are the regions associated with storing memories on the basis of the emotional states connected to the memory and hence help in the trigger of reactions to the stimuli of these memories.

Hypnosis For Anxiety

Most of us are anxious about something in our life. It could be being forced to talk to a crowd or driving or maybe even death. Even the most rational human being has something that they dread. Anxiety is more common phenomenon than you think. It usually results in sweaty palms, pounding heart, nervous feelings, tingling feelings in the stomach and even dizziness. To people who suffer from anxiety, the world shrinks down to just them and their problem. The fear seems indestructible even if it is just imaginary. In their minds, the fear is real so the symptoms of anxiety are also real. Hypnosis is a way to drive away these fears and anxiety attacks. The whole mind-over-body effect can be tapped into by using hypnosis or self-hypnosis.

Here are the steps to follow to use self-hypnotism to relieve the anxiety:

✓ Ensure that you are in a completely quiet room. Switch off all phones, computers, pagers, media players, etc. Also ensure that there is minimal noise from outside such as traffic or neighbors yelling.

✓   Now, find the most comfortable chair, recliner or bed in the room. Comfort is an essential part of the relaxation process. You can even use pillows or a thin bedcover if you feel uncomfortable or cold.

✓   Look around and choose three things that are there around you and recite it out. For example, there is a vase on the table next to the bed. There is a mirror on the opposite wall. The walls are pink. Telling yourself such statements will reassure your subconscious mind that you are not tricking it and that anything you say will be true. It makes it easier for your subconscious mind to believe in the hypnosis process.

✓   Close your eyes and think of a feeling that soothes you. It can be an oil massage or a nice hot shower.

✓   Now that you have that image in your head, imagine that this soothing feeling is flowing all over your body from your head to your toes. To take it a step further, you can imagine that wherever this oil flows, it leaves behind a warm or cool sensation, depending on preference and season.

✓   Now, imagine that you are in front of a blackboard. Pick up a chalk of a color you like and a new eraser.

✓   Start writing numbers starting from 100 going backwards. Write them big and slowly. After you write a number, erase it completely, take a deep breath to relax yourself and then write the next one.

✓   If you feel extremely stressed out or anxious, you can even attempt a more complicated mind game by writing only odd or even numbers.

✓   This mind exercise will allow you to temporarily forget your worries of the day and instead focus on the blackboard inside your mind.

✓   Once you feel completely relaxed, look for a white door in your mind's eye. Open the door. On the other side of the door you'll find the most beautiful place you have ever seen. What this place is will depend on what soothes you at the time of the hypnosis. It could by a white sand beach or a lush forest or maybe even just a room with a huge bed. There will be tiny details that will be specific to what you always wish for in such places such as a hammock or a garden or maybe hidden passages or even a stack of your favorite books.

✓ Just allow yourself to pass through the door into the wonderland beyond. Just feel yourself sink into the sand or the green grass and take in the beauty around you. All these are to help you disconnect from the world around you. You will find that your subconscious adds its own sensory stimuli such as smell and touch.

✓ This is what self-hypnosis allows you to do. Create a place in your mind that allows you to control the pain and stress you feel. You have the capacity to create an escape that relaxes not just your mind but also your body. It allows you to take back control of the one thing you lose in a stressful or anxious situation, your mind!

✓ Remember that this state of control cannot be achieved in just a single session. It takes a lot of time and patience to achieve a perfect self-hypnosis session. Practice it regularly so that it will be easier for your mind to reach this positive state.

✓ If you plan to perform the hypnosis on other people then you should be able to guide them to their perfect place using just your voice. Make sure that you voice is soothing and calm because any change in tone could cause a disruption in the hypnosis.

Tips For A Better Self-Hypnosis Session

While performing self-hypnosis, it is necessary to be able to create new feelings and connections that you can carry out with you after your session. However, it will take a few tries to get your mind used to the whole process and for it to actually make a difference in your beliefs. Here are some tips to help make the process more effective.

✓   Create an anchor point on your body

An anchor point is a specific point on your body where if you touch it, it allows you to relax. Creating such a point in the body will make it easy for you to relax when trying to perform self-hypnosis. While creating an anchor point, think of a specific person or place or memory and imagine that you were at that place or with that person. Focus on the soothing feeling and touch the anchor point while telling yourself loudly but calmly how relaxed you feel. When you want to enter this relaxed state, close your eyes and touch your anchor point and count backwards from 10 and similarly when you want to wake up, count backwards again and open your eyes.

✓ Change your relationship with your anxiety trigger

Once you have entered the trance state of relaxation, it is time for you to change the associations you have made with the things that trigger your anxiety attack. Try to imagine the thing that makes you anxious in a funny way. For example, if you are scared of spiders, picture the most horrible looking spider and then forcibly change that image to something funny, say the spider being on roller skates and slipping all over the floor. The idea is to take something horrible and make fun of it so that your mind now associates the funny thing with that object, place or situation instead of the horrible one that causes your anxiety attacks. Keep practicing till you can feel a positive feeling when you think of or see the object again.

✓ Replace the negative belief

You could also try to prepare yourself on what the actual cause of your anxiety is by writing a diary where you explain your thoughts and feelings. When read these at a later time they could possibly give you insight into what situation or object gives you anxiety and why. After you identify the feelings, think about what you could believe in to make the situation a positive one. If you know this, it could make it easier for you to focus your mind on replacing the negative feelings during the hypnosis session. Once you identify a positive feeling for the situation, it becomes easier for you to concentrate on those during the self-hypnosis sessions and those will hence make you feeling calm.

✓ Listening to a recording

This method can even be used independently without the use of hypnosis. First, make a list of all the positive attributes you have, even something trivial like waking up early. Once you have a nice long list, make a recording of you saying those attributes gently but reassuringly. It should be in a convincing tone, yet at the same time sound decisive. Make sure your sentences end with a definite full stop instead of sounding like questions. For example, 'I am in control of my feelings.' rather than 'I am in control of my feelings?' Also try to avoid negative phrases or double negative phrases like, 'I will not get stressed.' Instead use positive ones such as 'I will remain calm and composed.'

Making the sentences sound positive will play a key role in the relaxation of the mind. You could listen to these when you sleep or even during hypnosis if somebody else is assisting you with the process.

Practicing hypnosis and self-hypnosis at regular intervals will ensure that you retain the ability to remain composed and calm through almost any situation that might arise. It allows a sense of tranquility to prevail over your mind and body. It improves your mental health and hence your physical health as well. It is found that, being calm and relaxed can also improve your relationships with the people around you.

Hypnosis For Depression

Depression is a state of mind wherein a person feels 'low' and has an aversion to activity even ones needed for basic survival. This can affect a person's thoughts, feelings and actions to an extent where the person can feel so depressed that they can't even make themselves get out of bed. Almost everybody faces some amount of depression in their life. For some people the depression is associated with a particular event or stage in life. So once that passes, they become their normal selves again. However, for others it is a chronic depression that never truly leaves them and reappears frequently in their lives.

Depression is often a defense mechanism of the mind to a past traumatic or abusive event. The 'traumatic triggers' are either the people or situations that we associate with the trauma. An example of such a situation or person could be when a loved one passes away. When someone close to you, be it a parent, sibling, spouse or friend passes away the trauma of living without them or if they live with you, clearing out their belongings can be trauma triggers that lead to the onset of depression. Some people find it so difficult to deal with the death of a loved one that they move from anything or anyplace that reminds them of the person they lost. Depression also forms in people who don't fully grieve for the person they have lost. Other triggers could be loss of a job, bankruptcy, divorce, lack of friends or sexual abuse.

The Signs Of Depression

Most people fail to observe the obvious signs of depression in their friends and family simply because they aren't aware. People just pass it off as grief or 'just a bad day'. Even the actual sufferers don't pay heed to the starting symptoms of depression. If they did, they could have sought help at the beginning instead of letting the depression reach a stage when it became part of them. Here are some of the common signs of depression that might slowly creep onto people without them even being aware of it unless they are actively looking for it.

✓ Feeling lethargic

Sometimes you could feel lethargic and lazy to such an extent that you have no interest in doing anything. You would just not want to move from the bed. Most people just put that down to a general laziness or maybe the weather but it could be something more than that. It could be a sign that your mind is extremely tired and is shutting down emotionally.

✓ Worry about diseases

People who suffer from depression tend to experience a physical manifestation of the mental trauma in terms of body pain or mild diseases. To add to this, even the slightest cold will worry you to the extent that you will feel like you are contracting a major illness such as arthritis or cancer or diabetes.

✓   Indulging in bad or unhealthy habits

Sometimes to cope with the depression, people turn to bad habits or even unhealthy ones. Some might start drinking on a daily basis or smoking to find a relief from all the sadness. Others might take to overeating, especially sweets and chocolates while others stop eating. Some take to drugs such as marijuana. All these are coping mechanisms but of the wrong kind.

Insomnia

Insomnia is a common complaint amongst people suffering from depression. The constant feeling of depression causes the mind to worry and work overtime resulting in insomnia.

✓   Feeling emotional

With your mind in a disturbed state, it is only natural that your emotions will be all over the place too. People who suffer from depression often feel like crying for no reason at all or they feel like the world is against them or hurt. But most of the time they just feel empty and lifeless. They feel like there is nothing worthwhile in this life. This is when they possibly become suicidal.

Most of the times, these symptoms are treated with medicines such as anti-depressants; sleep medication, diet program, smoking or alcohol rehab centers, etc. These methods deal with the symptoms but not the problem. Stopping the drinking isn't going to make a person free from depression unless the alcohol is the source of the depression. Hence these treatments only cure or stabilize the symptom rather than the cause of the depression. If the person suffering from depression goes to a counselor where they can talk about their feelings instead of just popping pills, it is possible to get to the root of the problem and then treat that rather than treat the symptoms.

While companies will lead you to believe that medications will help, they are filled with side effects. This is where hypnosis comes in. Hypnosis has been recognized as a possible therapy for people suffering from depression. While it doesn't have a 100% success rate, it is worth considering hypnosis as a form of treatment for people suffering from any form of depression. Hypnosis is useful not only for discovering the underlying cause for the issue but also help people cope with the problem. Hypnosis helps you achieve a generally happier disposition and decreases your tendency to sound pessimistic or negative. Instead of staying in the loop of negative thoughts and feelings of uselessness, hopelessness and guilt, hypnosis allows you, as a person, to break loose from the incessant cycle of negativity and gain a more positive outlook in life. Instead of going through life with the thought that something bad happened to you, hypnosis will help you cope with the horrible past and move past it into a better present and future.

In most cases, but not all, depression stems from a traumatic or abusive event in the past. Hypnotherapy can be used to help the person react differently to the painful situations or memories that bring on their bout of depression. It can also help them become aware about the cause of their depression and help them let go of the painful memories and feelings. These painful emotions can be replaced with more positive ones that will act as a step forward towards recovery. It ensures that the person becomes less vulnerable to similar situations and aids them in reacting in a much more positive manner.

In a hypnotherapy session, the therapist basically uses positive affirmatives and thoughts to help bring you out of your depression. These suggestions are made when you are in a state of relaxed mind. For example, sentences such as "I am happy with my life" or "I am a worthwhile person who is loved by friends and family" are some of the statements that can bring about a difference in the mental outlook of a person. While being put under hypnosis isn't a difficult task, it makes it easier for you if you feel at ease with the therapist. Trusting them and feeling relaxed around them will make it easier for them to perform the therapy and you will also respond faster. Hypnotherapy hardly elicits the same level of response in everybody. For some people, they start showing signs of improvement within the first few sessions while others take much longer. All these depend on the degree of trauma that you have faced and how much your mind has regressed after the unfortunate event. People who have borderline depression will obviously respond faster than people with a long duration of chronic depression. Many factors play a role in the effectiveness of the therapy including how willing you are to undergo the treatment, the relationship you have with the therapist and so on. Children tend to respond much faster than adults because they are generally more trusting and their minds are fresh and open to new ideas.

If you are considering hypnosis them you can consider various methods of delivery of the treatment such as through a therapist or self-hypnosis or maybe even CDs. One caution while using self-hypnosis is that you might not be able to be strong enough to continuously revisit the memories willing and change them which is why it is always better to have a therapist perform the treatment on you. CDs are also quite useful in terms of helping you cope with the depression but they aren't tailor-made to each individual's situation. No two people have the exact same issues so CDs might not be as useful as going to an actual therapist. CDs can be used as a supplement to a regular therapy session by a certified hypnotherapist.

How Does Hypnosis Helps Treat Depression?

✓   It allows you to deal with the subconscious mind. The conscious mind is just 10% of the subconscious mind so when we deal directly with the subconscious mind, it is a treatment of a 100% rather than just the symptoms that manifest in the conscious mind. It allows for faster and more complete healing.

✓   It allows you to identify the source of the problem. It helps identify the so-called 'unfinished business' that you may have, be it the loss of a job, loved one or home. This 'unfinished business' leads to the presence of residual feelings of regret, guilt, pain, sorrow, anger and fear which have no way to escape from the body. When these are not released soon after the traumatic event, they just get buried under a sea of numbness. The mind tries to repress the feelings to make them go away because it's easier to do that than deal with the residual feelings that are left behind.

✓ Hypnotherapy will help in the removal of these residual feelings. If these are left as such it can create a cycle of negative thoughts and reactions to any situation that reminds you of the trauma and the depression will never go away. Hypnotherapy takes you down to the deepest part of your mind that is where these memories and feelings are likely to be buried. Once there, the therapy will help you deal with these feelings so that they get released and you no longer have that feeling of hopelessness. Once the entire treatment is complete, you will be able to live a life free from those repressed feelings.

✓ It replaces the repressed feelings and the trauma with positive thoughts and emotions. Hypnotherapy aims at replacing the negative feelings with positive ones so that in the end the general feeling surrounding the event is one of positivity rather than negativity. With each session, the therapy aims at replacing the thoughts and emotions that debilitate you with ones that life you up and add some positivity to your life. At this stage, it is useful to use positive affirmations because the cause of the problem has been targeted and solved and only the symptoms are left to be healed.

✓   It creates a long-term improvement. Hypnosis is a treatment option that gives a long-term cure for depression. If the therapy is performed properly by a certified therapist, the effects are extremely beneficial. Hypnotherapy can be used not only to clear the mental issues but also to resolve the physical ones. Once the mind has been cleared and the source of the problem tackled, hypnotism can be used to improve the wellbeing of the person. It is widely used in correcting sleep patterns, lethargy, pain, headaches and libido. It works even better when these symptoms are the side effects of a problem in the subconscious mind.

Self-hypnosis can also be used in the place of conventional hypnotherapy. During self-hypnosis a person is forced to confront his traumatic experiences at various levels in his subconscious mind. As you go into a hypnotic state, you can introduce positive thoughts in your mind to nullify the negative ones that were formed along with the trauma. You can perform this therapy through meditation, imagery or relaxation techniques. To be able to practice self-hypnosis on yourself, you will first need to have a strong desire and will power to overcome your depression. Also make sure that you get in touch with a therapist who can advise and guide you before you perform self-hypnosis.

Hypnosis For Stress Relief

What Is Stress?

There isn't an actual medical definition for stress. Rather, it is a range of emotions we feel when life doesn't go the way we want it to. The emotions could be as slight as disappointment or irritation or it could even be a mental breakdown. We all experience stress at one point or the other in our lives. It can be due to problems in our professional or our personal lives. Each person copes differently to stress.

Stress can either hinder or aid a person depending on that person's threshold. Some people do their best work under stress while others breakdown under stressful conditions. People who are hindered by stress usually develop a number of physical and psychological problems due to it. Stress can cause a number of health problems as a way for our body to defend itself from the effects on stress on our brains. However, this means the release of excess energy that has nowhere to go because there isn't any physical threat so all this energy gets released as depression, anger and fear. If these feelings are not dissipated then it greatly affects our mental health and ultimately physical health. It can lead to headaches, high blood pressure, insomnia, ulcers, etc. This is why it is essential that you find a way to treat your stress and the related problems as soon as possible rather than brush it off as not a very important thing.

Most of us adapt to deal with a certain amount of stress on a daily basis. However, these stresses are usually trivial and easily dealt with. It is easy to just move on and get on with your life. However, chronic stress caused by a strained relationship or job stress, is both physically and emotionally draining. Most people who suffer from stress always complain about being tired. This is because they spend a lot of energy focusing on the source of their stress. Once you reach the stage where you feel that the stress is controlling your life, it becomes a 'stress disorder'. This disorder can be very devastating and prevents us from fulfilling our obligations in both our personal as well as professional lives. In most cases, people don't even consider stress to be a disorder worth getting treated for. They just assume that it will go away on its own. They realize way too late that they need to seek some help for it.

People have their own stress triggers. What stresses out one person need not necessarily cause stress in another person. The most common causes of stress are the imaginary ones because our brain can't distinguish between real and imaginary stresses in our lives. There are a number of common causes for stress including:

✓   Change

✓   Big changes like relocation to a new city or new school or a new house are often triggers for stress. While some people accept it as a new adventure and challenge, others get all stressed out about the change.

✓   High amount of pressure

When some people are put in environments with a high pressure, they tend to break down because they can't work or live in such environments. For example, if some students are put in a school where they expect everybody to get above a 90%, they tend to perform their worst because mentally they are constantly worried about whether or not they will do well.

✓   Not having a fast paced life

Some people tend to get stressed not about how their life isn't the way they envisioned it to be. Instead of an active life with lots of friends, a good job, frequent socializing if they have a boring, mundane life it can cause stressful conditions because they don't live up to their own ambitions.

✓   Having a lot of responsibilities

Sometimes people feel trapped by the responsibilities they have to shoulder and this could make them lead stressful lives because to them even if a single thing goes wrong, it just adds more burden to the already existing load.

✓   Not being in control of the situation

Some people get stressed out that they can't control a particular aspect of their lives, this only leads to them spinning even more out of control because they are now focusing on the stress rather than their lives.

Different situations in our lives can cause different levels of stress depending on a set factor such as how we perceive the situation, our emotional strength and our ability to deal with pressure. Our perception of situations is based on our experiences in the past, our thought process and the amount of self-confidence and self esteem that we have. Our emotional strength is based on how much of negativity or bad feelings we can handle without breaking down. The more resilient you are, the more likely you can withstand any stressful situation. Finally, how we deal with the pressure is basically how we use our skill set to deal with the problem and move on. Each person is different, so what situation is comfortable for you might be extremely stressful for another person. For example, there are some people who love meeting new people and being social, whereas there are others who dread going to parties or social gatherings because they are too shy to talk to anybody new.

Sometimes people even get stressed out about happy events such as a wedding or a new, better job because these things bring about change and uncertainty into their lives and they don't know how to handle it. To add to that, when everybody else is happy they feel obligated to be happy too, which adds onto the existing stress of change.

Symptoms Of Stress Disorder

Stress leaves its marks on your mind and body. You may exhibit signs of emotional, behavioral and physical changes that can be attributed to stress disorder.

Emotional Symptoms

Emotional symptoms of stress disorder usually include a wide range of emotions from anger and frustration to despair and depression. It can also lead to severe mood swings, especially at a time when the stress is at its peak. Unfortunately, these symptoms thrive on one another, so when one emotion arises, it often leads to the surfacing of other feelings as well. And by the end of it, you will only feel more stressed out than when you started because all these negative feelings will cause you to blow the problem out of proportion and make it look bigger than it actually is.

Behavioral Symptoms

When you become stressed, your behavior automatically changes. You tend to lash out at people or snap at them. You could even become moody and withdrawn or become increasingly defensive of everything you do or say. Insomnia is a common behavioral response to stress. You would have been the kindest, most mild-mannered person before you became stressed but once you are under stressful conditions you could become an angry, bitter person.

Physical Symptoms

Stress doesn't only cause changes in your emotions and behavior, it all elicits chemical changes in your body that lead to those emotional and behavioral changes. Consider your 'fight or flight' chemicals such as adrenaline and noradrenaline. These chemicals cause increase in blood pressure, heart rate and rate at which you sweat. These also reduce blood flow to the skin and stomach activity. Cortisol leads to the release of fat and sugar into the body and also thwarts the working of the immune system. These changes lead to the choice of flight or fight. However, they aren't very useful in stressful situations where you can't change a thing around you. For example, if there is a huge traffic jam and you are going to be late for a very important meeting. If you had left home late, then you can blame yourself. But what if the cause of the traffic pileup is an accident that happened? The situation is out of control. You can't fight nor can you run away. So, even though these chemicals are produced your body has no use for them. So they accumulate in the body and lead to changes that could possibly spoil your health if it happens often. As a result of these chemical accumulations, you could start getting stomach pains, headaches, nausea, high breathing rate, ulcers, etc. Over a long duration of similar situations, it could even lead to heart attacks and strokes.

How To Deal With Stress

Stress is considered to be the main cause for working professionals falling sick. The aim should always be to try and cope with the stress rather than eliminate it completely. If you manage the stress effectively, you can then use it to help you improve in life.

Here are some tips to help you deal with stress:

✓   Be well prepared for any stressful situation. For example, if giving a speech is your stressful event, then make sure you prepare well in advance so that the even goes off smoothly. This will help you feel less stressful about speeches in the future.

✓   Try to bring some positivity into any stressful situation. Tell yourself that a change in a good thing and isn't necessarily a threat to life as you know it.

✓   Try to make an active effort not to worry about events that are beyond your control. There is no point in worrying about an impending thunderstorm or a traffic jam caused by an accident because you have no say in when and where such things happen.

✓   Set achievable goals so that you feel good about yourself. There is no point in setting goals that are almost impossible just because you feel like you aren't aiming as high as anybody else.

✓   Ensure that you eat properly and healthy. There is no point in binge eating to compensate for the stressful feeling nor is it necessary to starve yourself. Eat healthy because it not only makes your body function properly but it also improves your mental wellbeing.

✓   Ensure that you get enough sleep everyday. Around six to eight hours of sleep is essential for a well-balanced mind and body. It doesn't help in stressful situations if your body and mind are exhausted from lack of sleep.

✓   Make it a point to exercise regularly, even if you aren't overweight because exercise releases the 'feel good' chemicals, Endorphins that make you feel better about yourself. They put you in a happy mood because they trigger a positive feeling.

✓   Don't hesitate to ask for help from friends, family or therapists. There is no shame in admitting that you have a problem, especially to friends and family. So go ahead and confess to them if you feel stressed about something. Sometimes, even just talking about the stress trigger might make you feel better.

Techniques That Help In Stress Management

There are a number of techniques that can be used in stress management:

✓   2 minute Relaxation

Focus on your breathing. Inhale and exhale slowly. Try to imagine a sense of calm spreading through your body as you breathe in and out. Try to loosen up the areas that are tense. Relax your neck and shoulders by rotating your head. Shake your hands and legs to release the tension in them. Think of some happy memories. Do this for around two minutes and you will automatically feel calmer.

✓   Relaxing the mind

Close your eyes and make sure that you inhale and exhale through your nose. Every time you exhale, say a single word or a short phrase such as 'okay' or 'I feel good'. Do this for at least five minutes. If you feel your mind wandering, then turn your focus to your breathing and your word or phrase. You can make the word or phrase as vague or as specific as you like, whichever helps you focus better.

✓   Changing behavior

If you take an active effort to change your thoughts and behavior, you will find that it is easier for you to cope with stress. If you start eating healthy, exercising, socializing, not take hasty decisions it will be easier for you to deal with any stressful situation that comes your way.

Treatment For Stress Disorder

Psychotherapy, counseling and hypnotherapy are effective therapies for stress. Cognitive Behavioral Therapy can also shed some like on the whys and hows of stress disorder. In stress disorder it isn't the situation itself that is responsible for the stress, rather how we react to the said situation. If it was the situation that was the cause, then a single situation would put everybody under stress but not everybody feels stressed about the same situation. By using hypnosis to alter the reaction to the situation, you can effectively combat stress.

Let's look into hypnotherapy as a possible treatment of stress. A hypnotherapist may be able to help you identify the source of your stress and from there you can work on the problem together so that you can relieve yourself of the stress. The cause could be a past issue or a bad memory that is coming back to haunt you at times that remind you of the situation.

Once you identify the source of the problem, you and your therapist can decide on a plan of action with an achievable goal in sight. Then you can work towards this goal. The goal should essentially include how you would like your feelings to change and what you want to accomplish in life without having to feel that stress is holding you back. The therapist will help you achieve these goals using a variety of techniques. Hypnotherapy starts showing its effects after the initial few sessions. For some people it might take longer because of various reasons. Maybe they aren't too comfortable with the type of treatment so they tend to put up barriers unconsciously in their mind. The barriers make it more difficult for you to reach the source of the problem and that's why for some people it takes longer. It also depends on the severity of the problem and the rapport you have with your therapist. It is a gradual process so it will take some time before you are completely healed.

Self-hypnosis

Self-hypnosis is known to be as effective as hypnosis in stress management. Here are the steps you should follow if you want to perform self-hypnosis at home.

✓   Find a quiet room that is free from distractions. Ensure that you keep all phones on silent and preferably practice it when you are alone or at least tell everybody else not to disturb you.

✓   First get into a comfortable position. Feeling comfortable is an essential part of feeling relaxed. Maybe sit on your favorite chair or lie down on the bed.

✓   Make each session about a goal. Choose something specific and small to start off with. For example, if you want to become calmer then focus on that for this session or if you want to reduce your stress levels then work towards that. Your subconscious mind focuses on positives as easily as negatives so thinking or repeating something positive can only help in achieving your goal.

✓   Take deep breaths to calm yourself down. As you breathe in imagine that the calmness is spreading throughout your body, from head to toe. Also imagine that as it is moving down, it is taking the stress away with it.

✓   Close your eyes. Imagine yourself to be in a calm environment. Any place that calms you down. For example, maybe a deserted beach or just a lush grassland or maybe even your own backyard. Focus entirely on this environment. When you are completely focused, it will be as though you are in a daydream.

✓ Once you are comfortable in your imaginary place, think of a positive statement and repeat it to yourself slowly. You can either say it out loud or think it. The point is that your brain should now focus on that phrase. Make sure the sentence is a definite one instead of ending in a question mark. Try to visualize the phrase or the outcome of the phrase. All this will help reinforce positive thoughts in your mind.

Comparison Between Hypnosis And Other Methods

Hypnosis requires more practice and skill than the other medicinal treatments or mind exercises. Hypnosis also requires some professional training or the presence of a trained therapist. However, hypnosis is useful for people who can't perform other treatments such as yoga due to physical and other medical restrictions. Hypnosis also has no negative side effects, which makes it better than medicinal and herbal treatments. And the main difference between other therapies and hypnosis is that hypnosis offers benefits that reach beyond a single disease. Medicinal treatments are specific for the mental disorder while hypnosis can be used for any kind of disorder. With a little bit of training, almost anybody can use hypnosis to successfully treat their depression or stress or anxiety.

Benefits Of Hypnosis

The most attractive aspect of hypnosis is that it can be used for the treatment of almost anything from stress to pain during childbirth. The added bonus that it has no negative side effects and is inexpensive also makes it a popular treatment option. It is also easy to learn and perform on one's self hence people can even practice it at home as a simple relaxation technique.

Drawbacks Of Hypnosis

Hypnotism is often wrongly considered to be a control-gaining tool. The fact is hypnotism cannot be performed against anybody's consent and it isn't done like how they show it in the movies with a pendulum hanging in front of your eyes. However, a vast part of the public are wary of hypnosis and this leads to problems during treatment.

When you aren't confident in the method, it becomes difficult for you to lower your barriers and enter the trance-like state of mind. Some people have a difficult to moving past their traumas while others can't find the focus for the hypnosis to work. If you can't focus on the positive phrases it becomes difficult for you to change your emotions, thoughts and feelings. Other people don't have the time to wait for the treatment to work. Hypnosis isn't an overnight solution. It requires patience and time that some people find hard to give.

Fred McGuaghy

Chapter 3
Repressed Memory

There is an awful lot of speculation about how treatments of the mind for repressed memory work but one should be aware that hypnosis has been criticized by many as being too suggestive in nature to accurately record things that someone has repressed. Experts argue that the repression is a deliberate attempt to put something very unpleasant out of one's mind and they are right. If something traumatic has happened to someone, they do know what that is, but may not be able to face it or put it into words, because it's easier to repress it than to face the demons. It's a very strange area. In the United Kingdom, for example, regression therapy in the form of hypnosis is not used in child abuse cases because of its seeming unreliability and the fact that facts recalled may be recalled by suggestion rather than actual memory. In the United States as well, repressed memory is usually dealt with by using therapeutic methods such as imagery and visualization, where a therapist deals with one patient on a one to one basis. What was found was that group sessions were also open to suggestion, leading to conclusions that were not thought to be completely accurate.

Thus, if you are facing a problem from the past that you have not been able to deal with such as grief, rape, child abuse or some kind of trauma that you cannot express, it would be wise to seek help from a specialist who deals with this problem individually by using visualization methods and guided imagery, though one has to be careful about the guidance given during guided imagery sessions. If you find a therapist that makes suggestions, rather than merely praises you for having remembered, be careful. They may actually be triggering memories of things that didn't happen by suggestion. Mind control is very easy to manipulate and in a situation such as this, where memories have been suppressed, the best way forward is to seek long term psychotherapy to discuss problems and to open the mind so that the patient is more willing to explore feelings and memories and gradually put sufficient trust in their therapist to come to conclusions that are of their own making, rather than having been suggested.

Grief therapy is something entirely different because what may have been repressed are emotions. The patient knows what the event was and that someone close to them died. Therefore going through hypnotherapy to bring out the grief isn't a bad idea and may help the patient to feel the emotions that they need to feel in order to move on. To my mind, having vast experience of this area, a bereavement counselor is a better idea because these are caring individuals who are specifically trained to deal with this particular problem and will know when to stop and when to pick up again on topics that are too painful for the patient to talk about.

Repressed memory is difficult to deal with in that there are so many different ways that professionals purport to deal with it. In the short term, psychotherapy helps because it may pinpoint what is going on in the mind and help to strengthen the patient's resolve to overcome the problems. However, there are no immediate answers and no definitive way to deal with repression of the memory. There are many services out there that purport to deal with repressed memory, though before venturing into this field, first look at the qualifications of the person offering the service. Then read up on what is being offered.

Recovered Memory Therapy is type of treatment to make people remember repressed or forgotten memories. It is often used in clients who have been abused as a child or people who have suffered a great trauma a long time back but have no memory of the incident. RMT is a controversial therapy with the mental health community divided on their opinion about the use of this therapy to awaken repressed memories. The researchers against RMT believe that any horrifying memory will be remembered all through the life of the victim. However, therapists and believers say that repressing memories is a common defense mechanism by brain when the mental trauma of a situation is too much for it to handle. According to these people, a child could suffer repeated abuse and yet not remember a thing while they could remember other happy times of their childhood. The more serious and frequent the abuse, the more deeply buried and repressed the memories will be.

Most therapists who use RMT believe that most mental disorders such as depression, eating disorders, insomnia, anxiety, and sexual dysfunction are caused by some sort of abuse during childhood. Memories of the abuse have somehow been repressed and the victim has no memory of the event even happening. Even though the abuse isn't in the part of active memory, it will still leave scars on the mind and lead to the disorders mentioned above.

When a person decides to visit an RMT therapist, it is because of partial images that the person is seeing that are confusing them. It is like seeing a movie with holes in the reel; you can see something but not enough to understand what is happening. Sometimes the patients don't have any sort of memory or flashbacks. In such situations they will be able to observe the bits and pieces as the sessions move on. Some people will be able to access them quite early in therapy while others will take longer. Through the various techniques that we will discuss presently, patients will be able to see parts of their memories like photographs until the entire memory is recovered. Further sessions help in the recovery of more scenes and in-detail facts about the memory.

Techniques used in RMT

Most therapists use a checklist that they compare with the symptoms that the client feels. If their symptoms are part of the checklist, they say that the client has a high chance of having some repressed memory.

To recover these memories, therapists use a wide variety of techniques including:

✓   Guided imagery

✓   Hypnotism

✓   'Truth serum'

✓   Dream work

✓   Age regression

✓   Automatic writing

Guided imagery is a technique that involves taking the client through an imaginary trip back to their childhood. The entire technique involves the use of words to guide the client back to a significant time in their childhood and make them recount whatever they felt. The idea is that rethinking and analyzing existing memories might slowly reveal the presence of a repressed memory.

Hypnotism is widely covered in this book and involves putting the client in a trance-like state where they are calm and relaxed and then talking them through their emotions.

'Truth serum' is the use of drugs to enhance memory power.

Dream work is the technique of analyzing dreams to see if any of them point towards abuse.

Age regression is taking the client back to their childhood memories and making them look for things they didn't notice at the time the memory occurred. It can also be coupled with taking the client to the location of their childhood, such as their parent's home or school or the playground.

Automatic writing is a technique where the therapists have the client write whatever comes to their mind with no filters or second thoughts. The writing doesn't have to be continuous nor does it have to be sensible, even random words are fine.

Most therapists claim to be able to recover memories of sexual abuse and/or incest during a person's childhood. The abuse is mostly perpetrated by a parent or sibling with the rest of the family members ignoring the abuse or not believing the child. In most cases, the abuse is frequent throughout the person's childhood. These memories are by far the most disturbing and damaging because of the fact that the perpetrators are most likely family or known people. It can lead to the destruction of familial ties. Abuse by unknown people causes less damage to a client's relationships because he or she can't blame them for the abuse.

However, there is a lot of controversy regarding the use of RMT and more researchers, therapists and public are gradually walking away from it. The main controversy is about how these recovered memories could be fake due to the impressionable techniques involved. If the memories are indeed fake or brought on by reinforcement or the misguided belief that there is abuse in the client's past, then it could do a lot of harm to the client and his friends and family. The client himself or herself gets affected by the memories and could spiral downwards into depression because of it. Families could get split up because of wrong accusations. In some cases it could even lead to suicide.

Fortunately, there is a way to differentiate an actual memory from a false one. False memories will seem out of the place to the victim and will often become less believable. If the memory isn't continuously reinforced, it could fade away. Also, even at the time of recovery, the memory will have gaps or things will seem out of place. Soon after these signs appear, people eventually decide that the memory is fake and reconcile with loved ones and move on with their life. However, some people realize it too late or never even realize it causing their lives to fall apart.

These techniques have been highly criticized so it is better if you think twice before trying this therapy out. However, there have been instances where RMT has been proven to bring out actual repressed memories in a person.

You may be better advised to let sleeping dogs lie and simply work on the problems that are facing you now, using professionals that understand the potential of past events being the reason for the way you feel and helping you to understand that connection without actually needing you to regress. Although some hypnotists do say that patients have been able to put their demons to bed by using regressive therapy, perhaps one needs to be aware that this may just bring about false memories and open more of a can of worms than merely going through traditional psychotherapeutic methods.

Chapter 4
Cognitive Behavior Therapy

Do you think that you cannot manipulate your mind into coping with chronic pain? You may actually be wrong in that assumption. Cognitive Behavior Therapy (CBT) is designed to help people who have to suffer pain long term and the way in which it does this is to look at each individual patient's coping skills, pain thresholds, the way that a patient perceives pain and helps the patient to regain control of their pain responses.

You may know people who have different pain thresholds and it's a common joke that men "die" over a bout of flu while women soldier on. There's a lot to be said for the way in which the mind perceives pain. People with a doom and gloom attitude toward pain will feel more pain because their brains are not able to release chemicals such as serotonin and norepinephrine – chemicals naturally released through positivity. Thus, without those chemicals circulating, the doom and gloom can set in and make people feel worse than they actually are.

Methods of CBT

Cognitive Behavior Therapy can be done in various ways such as: individual therapy, group therapy, self-help books or computer programs. Individual therapy essentially consists of one-on-one sessions with a therapist. These sessions are usually an hour long and a week or two apart. After the first initial therapy period of 20 sessions you would probably have to undergo a few booster sessions once in a few months. Group therapy can also be beneficial because of the mutual benefit of listening to other people's problems and how they tackle it.

When you are combined with a group of people who face the same problem, it becomes easier for you to relate to them and use their successes as inspiration and their failures as cautions for your own goals. Computer programs such as the Computerized Cognitive Behavioral Therapy (CCBT) are interactive software that plays the role of a human therapist. This type of therapy is also known as

Internet-delivered Cognitive Behavioral Therapy or ICBT. CCBT was started with the aim to reach out to the people who cannot access a human therapist either due to the lack of money or to the lack of an expert in their area. CCBT is in no way a form of learning over the Internet, it is a fully approved tool used to help people deal with the problems in their lives. There are a number of software programs that are available which will allow you to benefit from CBT with no contact from a therapist.

The main program currently being used by the NHS is known as 'Beating the Blues' and is approved for treatment of mild to moderate depression. CCBT is cost effective and has been shown to improve the conditions of patients with anxiety, depression and OCD. One study in the use of CCBT for the treatment of OCD in children showed that this type of therapy has a lot of potential amongst children and adolescent patients. CCBT is particularly useful to people who have a fear or insecurity of meeting other people. Self help books are also another way for you to overcome the problems you may face.

Exposure therapy is a form of CBT that is of particular use to people who suffer from Obsessive Compulsive Disorder

(OCD) or phobias. In the case of OCD and most phobias, talking will not be of much use to you and a more action-oriented therapy is necessary. This is where exposure therapy comes into play. Exposure therapy involves starting with the situations or objects that cause anxiety but a mild level of anxiety; one that you can tolerate. You need to remain in this environment for an hour or two or at least until the anxiety drops by half. It is better if you repeat this exercise three times a day. As you keep attempting this exercise you will find that over time your anxiety levels drop. Once you reach such a stage, you can move on to tackling other severely anxiety causing situations. The process continues till you have successfully conquered all the situations that you feel you need to conquer in order to overcome your OCD or phobia or even anxiety attacks. Exposure therapy needs at least 15 hours with a therapist. Alternatively, it can also be done using self-help books or computer programs.

How it works

CBT can't solve the problem for you but it can help you deal with the problem so that it is under your control. It gives you a sense of control in life and allows you to tackle it one step at a time. CBT is essentially broken down into:

- A situation

- Emotions

- Thoughts

- Actions

- Physical feelings

Each of these aspects affects the others and it is usually the situation that starts the whole cascade of your problem. From there, how you react to the situation can affect your thoughts and in turn your thoughts can affect your physical and emotional feelings and finally your actions depend on your feelings.

There are always two possible reactions to a situation: helpful and unhelpful. The unhelpful reaction is what steers you towards depression and other problems. CBT helps you to actively focus on trying to react in a helpful manner.

Let's consider an example:

On one of your bad days, you decide to take a small walk in a nearby park. On your way to the park, you see a friend of yours but she/he walks on, apparently, ignoring you. This situation could start a cascade of either a helpful or an unhelpful reaction. Let us take a look at the unhelpful reaction first. Your first thought is that he or she ignored me maybe they don't like me anymore. From this thought comes your first emotional feeling which are rejection and then the general feeling of sadness and 'low'. After this you will feel the physical pain such as headaches or lethargy or a fever. The ultimate thing will be you going home and ignoring them. You will constantly brood over it and make yourself feel worse than when you left the house. This will only lead to an actual drift between friends when there was none to begin with. This will only lead to more such bad situations and make you feel worse.

Now consider the helpful reaction. If your first thought is that maybe he or she is in a hurry or in some trouble, then your first emotion is concern and worry for your friend rather than sadness at being ignored. Such a feeling is positive which will lead to no physical manifestation. The only action you will take will be a positive one such as getting in touch with them to find out if something is wrong and this will only strengthen your friendship. As you just saw, the same situation can lead to two very different reactions that lead to drastically varying actions and events.

CBT can aid in creating this helpful reaction. It can help you alter the thought process of your mind that in turn affects your feelings and behavior. If you can change the way you perceive a situation, you can change the way you feel and the way you act. CBT aims at helping you tackle problems on your own in a positive manner without lapsing into a 'bad' thought or feeling. It aims to stop the negative cycles by teaching you how to deal with things that make you feel bad, anxious or frightened. By making it easier for you to deal with your problems, CBT helps you change your thought patterns and channelizes your energy into a more positive flow of thought. CBT can help you live life on your own terms without the help of a therapist.

What happens during a session?

Cognitive Behavior Therapy usually involves sessions with a therapist once in a week or two. The course of the therapy will be around two-dozen sessions with each lasting about half an hour or an hour. During these sessions you will focus on breaking down your problems and analyzing them at each step. The therapist will then help you realize which ones are unhelpful and how it affects your emotional state of your mind. Your therapist will also be able to suggest tips or ways to help you work out the bad thoughts and change them into useful ones. Once you identify the issue and plot a plan to reverse it, your therapist will probably ask you to implement the said plan in your daily life and the next session will probably deal with how those plans worked. The ultimate goal is to tell you how to implement the skills you learnt during therapy into your daily life and manage your problems to prevent them from having a bad impact on your life.

During Cognitive Behavior Therapy, you will be asked to work with a professional and to keep records. Of course, the homework that you are asked to do helps the therapist to establish what is causing most of your pain. This may be note taking and keeping a record of when the pain is at its worst. One particular case I can cite here was an elderly woman who had unbearable pain that became worse when it was nighttime. What seemed to be causing the pain was the fear in her head of being alone and dying. Thus, when that was dealt with, the patient found that her pain levels went down. The title of this book begins with the words "mind control" for a purpose. With this kind of treatment, a patient is able to take more control over the way that they see their pain in relation to the way that emotional response affects that pain. In the old woman's case, she was able to discuss her fears and with modern technology was set up within her home with an alarm that she could use in the event of being ill in the night. Just having that pendant within reach of her hands improved her health enormously and the psychological impact of that improvement was enormous. She no longer feared being alone and dying because she didn't actually feel alone anymore. Her lifesaver around her neck became her friend. In another case similar to this where a patient was unable to fend for herself, the therapist found that the suggestion of having a pet was something that was useful to the patient. Being a very caring person, other than for her own needs of course, the lady took the advice and found that she began to be more mobile because psychologically, she knew that the pet depended upon it. The therapist was then able to suggest the patient work on the real problem that was one of self-esteem. The patient didn't think herself worthy of anything less than the pain that she was suffering. She didn't feed herself properly and she didn't take the exercise that she needed. With the help of therapists her pain levels went down considerably by understanding that the problem was one of negativity and self-esteem – rather than one of pain being so bad that she was living a life of hell.

Important aspects of CBT

CBT is different from most other psychotherapies because of its distinct structure. It focuses only on the issue at hand rather than focus on other things on sidelines. It is also highly pragmatic in the sense that it helps you identify certain problems and deal with each one separately. CBT also focuses on your life at the present rather than the past trauma. It deals with how to cope with your present day feelings and thoughts rather than the ones that existed at the time of the trauma. The most important aspect of CBT is the fact that the therapist will in no way command or order you to do something. Instead he or she will guide you in finding the solutions to your problems.

Benefits of CBT

✓   CBT is as effective as medicinal treatments in treating most health disorders and is particularly useful in cases where medicines haven't helped.

✓   When compared to other psychotherapies, CBT is the fastest acting and progress can be seen in just a session or two.

✓   The highly structured format of CBT allows it to be given as treatment in various formats including groups, computer programs and self-help books.

✓   CBT tips and strategies can be used in daily life to help you deal with any sort of stress and problems, even trivial ones. It can be practiced long after the treatment is complete because it has no negative side effects even with prolonged treatment.

Drawbacks of CBT

✓   The major drawback of CBT is that for it to work perfectly, you need to be a hundred percent committed to the process. A therapist can only help so much but if you don't take the initiative then it won't make your problems go away. The therapist can't fix the problem for you, they can only guide you.

✓   The treatment depends on your state of mind. If you undergo the treatment at a time when you are low, it might be difficult for you to focus and be motivated enough to go through with the treatment.

✓   For the short duration of the treatment, your life will be very hectic. It will seem as though your life revolves around this treatment and to an extent it will because you will be spending every spare minute either attending sessions or practicing it at home.

✓   Due to the structure of CBT, it isn't exactly suitable for people who are suffering from complex mental issues such as schizophrenia or people with learning disabilities. It isn't a suitable treatment for such disorders but it is much for effective for the milder mental disorders.

✓   It can make you feel uncomfortable or emotionally unstable because the treatment revolves around confronting your feelings and fears. This might make you extremely anxious and put you in emotional turmoil.

✓   Some critics of the treatment argue that since CBT only focuses on current problems and emotions, it does not necessarily address the cause of the mental condition, say a trauma or abuse so it cannot be a cure for the disorder rather it just helps people cope with it.

✓   CBT focuses on the individual person's ability to change their thoughts, emotions and behavior rather than deal with the wider issue that they face with a person or a situation. Nor does it involve the role that friends and family play in a person's life.

When one understands the theory behind Cognitive Behavior Therapy, this can be applied to all areas of their lives and they don't particularly need to go to a specialist every time a problem exists. Your mind is so powerful that you can take on this kind of treatment of your own life by introducing the following elements:

- Positive attitude and frame of mind

- Knowing how to respond to pain

- Learning how to control anxiety

- Learning to replace negative with positive

-

Once these responses are incorporated into your life, you learn that the physiology of the brain mechanism helps to release positive endorphins that make pain less. Thus, in a nutshell, you are responsible for your response to pain and can make it easier to bear even if you have a chronic and ongoing illness that causes you pain.

Chapter 5
The Power of Biofeedback

Do you have any idea how powerful this is? Believe me, it's one the best ways of making yourself feel wonderful about your health. What human beings need is control over their lives and with all the gadgets that we have available to us, we can actually get rid of the worry of health by using biofeedback techniques in the comfort of our own homes. Let me show you how, but one thing you have to promise is that you won't get neurotic!

The first piece of equipment you need is a wristband blood pressure gage. You can buy these from online stores. Try to get one with heartbeat on it because this helps too. You have to learn to listen to your body and not use these in times of panic. The problem with doing that is that you can become neurotic and make your blood pressure and heart rate rise if you believe that the reading says you have something wrong and that's not the idea at all. The idea is to use these as tools so that you can monitor your life and find out which things you do hurt you more and what you should avoid doing. They also help you to see which activities actually encourage the best results.

Before you start, find out from your general practitioner what your ideal blood pressure should be and write it down. Find out from him what your heartbeat should be and write that down too. I could give you an average chart of this but that's dangerous territory since every human being will have their own medical history that will dictate what these are. Thus, with your doctor knowing you, trust what he/she says. Making a note of it helps you to aim toward the ideal.

Another thing you can invest in for the home is a thermometer. This gives you feedback as to whether you have a fever or not. Often, when the body feels hot and sweaty people panic and in fact, they haven't even got a high temperature. Buy one with a smiley face on it when you are within normal parameters because these add to the fun of using them.

Taking Notes

This aspect of biofeedback is vital to making it work for you. The first readings that you have in your book are your ideal blood pressure and your ideal temperature and heartbeat rate. Every morning when you get up, sit on your bed and take your blood pressure reading and heartbeat reading. Write these down in your book and note next to them as follows:

Temperature	Heartbeat	Blood pressure	Time of day and activity level
36.5	86	130 over 80	Getting up from bed
36.8	96	140 over 90	After a walk

As you do this – and bear in mind that the above numbers are make-believe and are just filled in to give you an idea of how to make your chart – you will begin to see a pattern emerge. Keep this record because it's your biofeedback. It's useful for the doctor and it's useful for you, but in the next chapter, I am going to teach you to manipulate your biofeedback to your advantage.

Once you learn to do that, you actually change your activities to suit yourself as an individual. If this method of manipulation interests you, then read on. It's particularly good for people who suffer from anxiety attacks, fibromyalgia, rheumatoid arthritis and other similar illnesses, but it's also great for people who want to try and turn their lives around and make them more positive.

Chapter 6
Manipulating Your Biofeedback

To do this, you need to have kept records for at least three weeks. This gives you an overall view of what's good for your body and what's not good for your body. If your heart is stretched to beating too fast all of the time, you need to go for those activities that don't provoke that reaction. If your blood pressure is high during stressed times, then that must show you that you need to lessen the stress that you are suffering. It doesn't mean running to the doctor for the slightest ailment. You have the power to control your body's response to whatever it is that you are going through simply by adjusting your activities to those which give the best responses.

Exercises for those who are overstressed and have high blood pressure

Exercise 1 – Self-hypnosis

Try this experiment and see if it helps you. It uses hypnosis in a way that you may not have experienced it before. You need to buy yourself a hypnosis CD and there are loads available on Amazon.com and other outlets that sell CDs. These are usually labeled as being suited to those who are trying to find answers to stress. Self-hypnosis is usually performed lying down comfortably on the bed. You listen to the CD and concentrate on what is being said. Try to cut out all other thoughts. You may need to practice for a while, but what this will do is give you more control over your stress levels and thus help you to cut down on your high blood pressure problem, which may be being caused by stress related issues. By the way, if you have high cholesterol as well, make sure that you see your doctor regularly and eat a raw apple a day to try and bring these levels down as well because they may be the cause of the high blood pressure.

When you perform self-hypnosis, you should always make sure that you are going to be left alone during the whole session. You need to choose an ambiance that is calming and this is very important. Make sure that your clothing is loose and that when you lie down, your head is supported and you feel perfectly comfortable.

Exercise 2 – Relaxation exercise

This exercise is for those who don't like the idea of self-hypnosis but who want to feel the benefit of relaxation to help bring down their blood pressure levels or to calm down after getting particularly frantic in life. Lie down in a darkened room with no distractions. Make sure that you can't hear the TV or the kids in the next room. Wear comfortable clothing and relax you head onto a soft pillow. Place your arms at your sides and lie on your back.

Imagine your toes and without thinking of anything else at all, concentrate on them. Tense them and feel them tense. Slowly and purposely, let them relax until they feel heavy and move through all the parts of your body from the tip of your toes right through to the top of your head, doing the same thing – first tensing and then relaxing.

If you find that your mind wanders, force yourself to start again. The problem that is giving you all this high blood pressure or the feeling that you are out of control is the fact that your problems are becoming such that all of the chemicals that are usually released within the body when you feel good are not happening. Relaxation helps them to be released and gives your mind a break from the stressors that are causing you to feel so bad in the first place.

The above exercises are great for stress, unhappiness, anger, frustration and all the negative elements within your life and are thus going to make you feel more relaxed and able to cope. Before you go back into your world of chaos, sit slowly and let your mind get accustomed to slow movement. Don't rush back into the chaos and expect the relaxation or self-hypnosis to work if you just ignore what you have just done. Instead of doing that, take your time and let your body and mind adjust slowly. That way, you retain that feel good factor that you gained from doing the exercises in the first place.

Chapter 7

Creating Pain Levels

Often when you go to a hospital ER, you are asked to categorize your pain on a scale of one to ten. If you feel really badly, you will choose a number on the higher end of that scale and if the pain were not that fierce, then you would choose a low number. What if you could control the level of pain yourself in your mind? I have been doing this for years and it works. You have to concentrate to actually achieve it, so please try to follow the instructions below.

If you believe in your mind that pain affects different levels of your brain, then you can move up to another level when pain happens to stop the negativity of the experience and continue to allow serotonin levels to stay stable. You may think this is pretty incredible, but it works nonetheless, especially if you – like me – believe in it. The power of the mind is incredible and I got the idea from watching people who were carrying out near impossible feats under difficult circumstances. For instance, if you were injured in the desert and you knew that you had to get to shade to survive, you would make a superhuman effort to do just that whereas if you simply had to get somewhere to see a doctor, the same urgency isn't there. The superhuman ability to overcome pain and adjust to it is something you see heroes do every day of the week, so why can't individuals apply the same rules to their pain control. I control my mind when I am in pain because I don't believe in taking excess medications. I don't like what they do to my body, so the only alternative that I had was to find a way to make the pain less.

Coming out of surgery, for example, other people within the same ward that had undergone the same surgery as me were still in bed after four days. I had not only managed to get out of bed, but had moved sufficiently to make the pain much less while watching others demanding pain medications. I know this system works if you can bring yourself to believing in it.

Your mind is quite powerful. When you suffer a pain in your body, sit down. Instead of concentrating on the pain, close your eyes and try to think of the pain as being at a certain level within your brain. Remember, all messages from your body are sent through to the brain anyway – so tackling the pain in your brain area seemed to make common sense to me. Try to think of the pain – and then make a conscious effort to think above the pain. If you can think of your pain as being like different levels literally, you are able to move your thinking to a level above the pain.

As you can see, the initial pain is felt, but my moving your thoughts to another level and then adding positive thoughts, you overcome the pain and the pain seems less. At the top level where you are encouraged to think positive thoughts, here's an idea that works. Close your eyes, move yourself up to the next level and then use something called visualization to make the serotonin levels in your brain kick into action. Try to think of something in your life that was the most positive experience you ever had. Visualize how you felt, see the image of the event and let this be your third level because when you do that, you replace pain with actual positive reinforcement and the serotonin that is released from your brain helps your pain to go away.

Can I offer you any scientific evidence that this works? Perhaps. Let me see. The Harvard Medical School gave one answer, though there were thousands that I could choose from. You may think that information on this kind of pain control is scant, but believe me, it isn't. I discovered this method of pain control because I was forced to. At my age, the things that had happened in my past and my health were both playing a part in how I was feeling and I wasn't feeling that good. The alternatives left open to me from medical science made me question the validity of taking tablets. I argued that my body was trying to tell me something and that it was important that I recognized that I had pain – whether psychological or physical – and although it was like arguing with a brick wall, it worked for me. Pain medication or psychiatric medication wasn't an answer. What it turned out to be was like sticking a Band-Aid on a larger problem. Thus I had to find a solution. Look at this quotation from Harvard Medical School and you will see that they agree with me when they talk about pain.

"In those ways, it resembles depression, and the relationship is intimate. Pain is depressing, and depression causes and intensifies pain."

Thus, my way of coping with it takes the depressive element out of the picture and allows the mind to feel better. When you send messages to your brain that are positive, you take away the depressive nature of pain and start to let your brain see something positive and respond by letting all those positive chemicals come out to play. That's exactly what I do and what is being suggested here.

Have you ever seen the different ways that people respond to pain? We all have the same physiology and yet one person can respond to pain in a very different way to another. If what Harvard Medical School says is correct, it can therefore be assumed that if we let pain depress us, the pain will inevitably get worse. I know one lady with fibromyalgia who has to make everyone around her know that she has a pain. We actually nicknamed her as a "pain in the neck" because it's almost as if it's something that she uses to try and gain sympathy. I asked her one-day whether she actually drinks water and is was as if I was asking her whether she was born on the moon. She is letting her illness define who she is and I refuse to do that. Looking at both of us – and we are the same age – my years don't show up as much as hers because I don't let pain dictate who I am. If you apply the levels theory to your pain or to your stress or anxiety, you really can help yourself to recover and to feel very positive about life. Let me share the scene that I use as my positive reinforcement when I shift pain levels so that you can see the kind of thing that you need to use as your visualization of pleasure – so that your brain switches from thinking it's in constant pain to thinking that it's time to release serotonin.

My image is from my youth. I was 10 years old and won an award for a poem that I wrote and I remember standing up to get my prize. It was the first thing I had ever won in my life and it was a defining moment in my youth. It felt so good to have been picked out to win that award that I can picture myself going up to the front of the hall to collect it. I even see the scruffy clothes that I was wearing. In that moment in time, I didn't care about our poverty level or whether I looked a sight. All I cared about was that someone had recognized something positive in my writing and that was a wonderful feeling.

Make yours something that you know to be positive and something you know to have been a defining moment in your life and you can start to profit from mind control on your own terms like I do.

Fred McGuaghy

Chapter 8
Manipulating Self Esteem Levels

There are times in everyone's life when they feel like their self-esteem has taken a kick in the teeth. If you can take control of feelings of this nature from the moment that they happen, you may just avoid letting self-esteem issues get to such an extent that they make you miserable. I have a way of doing this because I have been at the point in my life when I felt that I was worthless and you don't get much lower than that. The teen years and the years of initial heartbreaks can do that and people can even let self-esteem issues follow them into adulthood, making their lives a total misery. Misery always loves company but company may not feel the same way. I learned in my early twenties that the best way to lose friends was to wallow in it. You may have heard yourself saying, "come on – pull yourself together," and then found yourself drowning in tears because you haven't quite worked out how to manipulate your self-esteem levels. Let me show you how you can achieve this and you don't actually need specialist help unless the levels are so low that you feel life as it should be is finished!

What you need is a reality check. You are breathing. You are a human being and if you are able to use your arms and your legs, you're pretty lucky really. One of the first things you need to do to raise self-esteem issues is to help someone who is worse off than you. I learned this from someone I thought was worse off than me. Crippled for life and in a wheelchair, this guy taught me a lesson I shall never forget. There I was, feeling sorry for myself and there he was – noticing that I was feeling sorry for myself – and he picked me up from my misery and told me to follow him. We had known each other through a hospital stay and I was confident about him being a sincere kind of person and what he did taught me a lot. He took me to a place where we could see the whole city beneath us. It was early evening. The sun was going down and we could see all the city lights start to twinkle. Here we were, sitting on a roof looking at the world and seeing how huge it was. In comparison, both of us seemed so small. He pointed out something I had never noticed in the city before. Over toward the horizon, you could see the wild land of the countryside beyond the city limits and I had never noticed the hills there before. It was stunningly beautiful. You may think this has little significance, but it has a lot of significance because somewhere inside of me, I suddenly realized that in comparison with everything that the world had to offer, we were like little tiny grains of sand and the way that we felt sorry for ourselves really didn't make the slightest difference to what the world offered us in exchange. I felt humble. Humility changes everything. It helps you to feel spiritually connected and when you are, self-esteem is something that's so far from your thoughts that it's almost like selfish indulgence. That visit adjusted my own sense of unimportance because in the order of things, I was neither important nor unimportant. I was simple a part of something much larger than me.

One of the places where you can feel this may be on a beach at sunset, or on top of a hill where the scenery is spectacular. Whatever you choose as your "spiritual awakening" place helps you to manipulate your self-esteem levels and gives you greater control over who you are and how you see the world. The only reason that you have self-esteem issues is because you spend too much time analyzing past events, people's treatment of you and insist on seeing yourself as bigger in the picture than you actually are. Once you see this perspective, you begin to celebrate life more and learn to give more than you have been doing. That guy gave me back my pride. He gave me back my ability to see beyond my own shortcomings and I appreciate him for that to this day.

To follow on from the lesson that he taught me, I signed up to help at a local hospice and suddenly saw people who I knew were in a much more unfortunate situation than I would ever be. These brave people have nothing to be brave about and yet their level of belief in life is astounding. They celebrate life more than people who could be enjoying years and years of happiness, even though they know that their time left on this Earth is limited. If that doesn't teach you something about needing to adjust your way of thinking, nothing will.

Chapter 9
Mind Control Over Anger

Anger uses up so much energy that it drains a human mind. It becomes so intense in its thoughts that sometimes your mind rushes out of control and you say words that you can never take back. So many people let that anger explode and break up relationships, betray trust and betray themselves simply because they have no idea how to control that negative aspect of their lives. The way to control anger is the same as controlling other negative feelings. Let's have a look at negative feelings that will harm who you are:

- Anger

- Pessimism

- Hatred

- Jealousy

- Greed

- Resentment

Some of these negative feelings come in progression. For example, if you feel jealousy, chances are that you also feel hatred and resentment as well as anger. If you feel hatred, you will also feel anger because hatred is a very strongly negative feeling that doesn't come about all on its own. Greed is when you feel that you are entitled to something that you really are not and often greedy people feel resentment toward those who have more than them. You can see from this that all these negative elements of human life are hand in hand and are ganging up on you. If you let them win – you become a very unhappy person. Let's try and demonstrate how it all accumulates to make you miserable.

A woman marries a man who doesn't want her to have a career. She is slightly resentful and sees herself as more than just a housewife. She doesn't really want kids and he does but she gives in. She then becomes a mother and puts off all her own ambitions to raise the kids. Though she loves her kids, she also resents them. They are the reason she never had the chance to do the things that she wanted to do in her life. Thus, when the kids disappoint her by not adhering to her plan for them, she reminds them constantly of the sacrifices that she has had to make so that they can have the things that she never achieved.

In a case scenario such as this, the woman is surrounding herself with misery and she is determined that those around her feel it too. She doesn't know it yet, but unless she can drop the negativity, she will turn into a very bitter old lady who hasn't really got any friends. Negativity bites away at who you are until there isn't much left. A person who suffers from managing anger is also letting himself start to experience the spiral that leads to total misery. Anger is negative. It's a trait that shows weakness rather than strength and if you want to adjust your behavior and avoid becoming an angry and unhappy person, you need to learn to control your mind, so that you see anger in a very different way. The first thing that you need to do when you feel anger is distance yourself from it. You may not immediately be able to take the anger out of your mind, but you need to distance yourself from what you see as the source of your anger. For instance, if the kids made you angry, go somewhere else in the house where you don't have to show them your anger. If your husband made you angry, go for a walk rather than letting that anger take a huge chunk out of his trust in you.

The second step with anger is to replace it with positive thought. The more you let anger fester in your mind, the worse the situation will get. Thus, you need to literally banish the anger and refuse to think about it. If there are things that you need to discuss with the source of your anger, this needs to be in a positive way or you gain nothing. Drop it and replace it by doing something that you enjoy doing. The reason you need to get these angry feelings out of your mind is so that your subconscious can work out the solutions all on its own. Believe me, if you give it the space to do that, it will come up with solutions that are positive and that do achieve results that work for everyone.

If you have problems with dropping anger, try affirmations that are positive if that works for you or alternatively, try to learn meditation because this helps you to control your mind with breathing exercises.

Meditation exercises for anger

Go to a calm place. Even the bathroom will be a good place where you can close the door behind you. Make sure you have a seat in there for occasions like this. Sit down. Close your eyes. Breathe in through your nose and don't think about anything else at all except the breath that is coming into your body. Hold your breath for a few seconds and then breathe out through the nose feeling the upper abdomen and stomach pivot while you breathe out.

It sounds very simple and it actually is. The hard part of it is letting go of the anger long enough to keep concentrating on your breathing. If you find yourself going back to anger, start again. You know when people try to put on a serious face to say something and have problems because they can't stop giggling, treat it like that. Put on your serious face and start again. Keep on breathing in and out in this way, thinking of absolutely nothing except your breathing. If you can keep this up for up to 15 minutes, you will find that by the time you have finished, you actually feel refreshed and may even have forgotten what it was you were angry about in the first place. Before you go racing downstairs to celebrate life with your partner or your family, take a deep breath and go back into your life slowly and calmly. Nothing outside the door has changed. You have and your attitude has. Let people who made you angry see that you are serene and composed. It will really help you to see how fruitless anger is and start to make you see the positive side of life, instead of exaggerating the negative side of life by giving in to anger. Be bigger than that anger. Be stronger than anger. Be ashamed of angry thoughts and replace them with the ability to stay calm. Everything will work out in the end. You just need to trust yourself and life a little more. When you do, you naturally adjust your positivity at the same time.

Chapter 10
Applying Therapeutic Psychology to Your Life

In previous chapters, we have discussed traditional therapeutic psychology where you take your lead from professionals. However, if you don't feel comfortable with seeing a professional and are sufficiently strong-minded, you can try therapeutic psychology of your own behavior by using analysis to help you overcome the obstacles that come into your life. It's actually a very logical process and in psychology, you may have things that you say mirrored back at you by professionals in an attempt to make you see that your way of looking at a situation is a little skewed and not always the most sensible way of looking at it.

Patient: I feel that my sister is going to kill any chance I have of being successful.

Psychologist: So you feel that your sister is hijacking your chances of success?

Do you see how they do it? They don't actually tell you what to do. They mirror the thought so that you can see it from another perspective and think to yourself "That sounds a little bit ridiculous," and often thoughts that you have while in a depressed or agitated state are ridiculous. However, what if you could do this alone? I am not suggesting that you stand in front of a mirror and talk to yourself although I have done that on occasion! What I am suggesting is analysis. If you have a scrapbook, you can start to draw down things that you think and work out why you think them.

I have written a very simple explanation about why you may not get on with your sister. It is by no means complete, but it's a chain of thought and as you do this you begin to work out where things go wrong, but the missing element in this way of analyzing things is that you haven't added empathy. Empathy is powerful and business executives and people who want to go forward in their lives use it so that they can understand the thoughts of others and incorporate these into whatever it is that they are planning. Look at the simple chart below:

The chart is too simplified, as it's unlikely that age is the only issue between you. You need to think about her as well and see things from her angle. For instance, you may think that she is favorite of your parents and your parents are always asking you to live up to her standards. That's a common complaint that people have about siblings who are more successful or academic. Now use empathy to see the picture more clearly. Her thoughts are likely to be that she wishes that mom didn't keep using her as an example. She may feel that she can't misbehave or have fun because mom and dad think she is so good. She's not getting a fair deal out of this either. Empathy helps you to see that. She may resent always being held up as the example of goodness because she actually wants to run barefoot across the park and do some of the irresponsible things you do naturally.

When you begin to analyze the whole picture, you get a much clearer idea of what's really happening. Write down your thoughts and resentments and then work them out from every angle there is. Why is mom so mean? Step into her shoes for a moment. Why is your boyfriend treating you badly? Look at the situation from his viewpoint. You begin to see a very different picture when you do this and it not only helps you to mature in the way that you see life, but it also makes you much more positive in your response to people and that means that you are able to deal with the hurdles that life puts into your path more easily. Empathy is a wonderful tool that anyone can incorporate into their therapeutic psychology because it gives a much fuller picture of what is actually happening in life instead of seeing things in black and white.

I remember as a teen thinking that the world revolved around me. Most teens feel like this because they haven't yet found out otherwise. Unfortunately, the world doesn't revolve around you and it shouldn't. When your world is as narrow as that and doesn't include analyzing the thoughts and feelings of other people, it's a very sad world to live in and you restrict yourself to seeing everything in tunnel vision.

When you use your scrapbook to write out a problem from all angles, you begin to see patterns and ways to change your world because you include everyone into the picture, rather than wallowing on self. This is the way you could be looking at your problem, based on the above.

My sister is in a horrible situation. She can't have as much fun as I can because my mom keeps setting her up as the perfect example of how to behave. I should be glad I can have the fun that I can and be a little more friendly toward my sister, trying to find out how I can help her have the fun she deserves.

Seen from this perspective the problem is very different indeed and you manage to open up your own perspective and encourage friendly connection between two people who may have appeared, on the surface, to have been rivals.

Fred McGuaghy

Conclusion

As you have read through this book, you have seen a variety of ideas that you can incorporate into your life to put you in the driving seat of your existence. I love being in control of my life, but it took me years to perfect this art that is why I took the time to write the book. When you have read it, keep it on your Kindle or on your bookshelf and refer to it from time to time when negative things happen in your life. You really are in control but only when you understand what being in control is all about.

You need to learn compassion, empathy, humility and kindness to others and to yourself. Once you do, you can use that to steer the course of your life in such a way that you really do control what happens within your mind and within your life. If you suffer from pain, there are exercises that you can do to help minimize it. They work and will help you to become a much more positive person. I have included exercises in relaxation that take a bit of practice to achieve. There are exercises in meditation, breathing methods and self-hypnosis. I have also included manipulation techniques that adjust your life when it goes off course.

If you do keep an analysis journal, it's a very worthwhile exercise because when you look back on the pages of analysis over the years, you can actually see your own growth looking back at you from the pages. I started mine at the age of 28 and 30 years later, it was still teaching me to keep on track. It was interesting seeing how narrow minded I used to be when I looked at the earlier pages of that book and how spiritually and mentally developed I have become through my own efforts. You too can achieve that level of competency and happiness if you set your mind to take in the positive aspects of life. You also need to drop all the negative aspects of your life because these are like anchors and tie you to the same spot until you can't move forward. Anger will harm you. Jealousy will tie your hands behind your back and greed will take your life and make it look absolutely futile. By taking control of all of these aspects of your life, you wake up in the morning and look forward to another day of making you and everyone around you shine in the best way that they can. People will want to be in your company. Your friends will respect and love you and you, in turn, will love yourself without letting self-love turn into vanity of any sort. In fact, life will change to such an extent that you will wonder why you didn't tackle life in this way years beforehand.

If I was to live my life over again, I don't think that I would tackle it in any other way. We all have to get through the quagmire before we start to see life clearly. Now that I do, the road that took me to this level of understanding has been a worthwhile road, regardless of the mistakes that I made on the way. If you have regrets, don't let them become resentments. If you have bad memories, don't let them overshadow the good memories. When you can put a bad memory out of your mind, it disappears very quickly, though if you keep precious memories in your mind to visualize instead, these become a part of who you become and that's very positive indeed. I hope that the lessons of my life have helped you to widen the scope of your life, though using hypnosis, mind control and by revamping the way that you look at life.

When you do revamp it, you are able to change everything that affects your life in a very positive manner. The aim of this book was to show you how I did it and to use my experience to illustrate how you can apply positivity to your life as well. Your manipulation of your mind and the way you look at life is essential. A thought is only in your mind while you allow it to be. Remember that, and the power that follows is amazing. You can drop negativity, feel less pain and wake up in the morning looking forward to another day with a new sense of optimism that makes life worthwhile.

Thank you for Reading! I Need Your Help…

Dear Reader,

I Hope you Enjoyed **"Psychology: Hypnosis & Mind Control – To Overcome Stress, Anxiety, Depression & Finally Recover Your Happiness"**. I have to tell you, as an Author, I love feedback! I am always seeking ways to improve my current books and make the next ones better. It's readers like you who have the biggest impact on a book's success and development! So, tell me what you liked, what you loved, and even what you hated. I would love to hear from you, and I would like to ask you a favor, if you are so inclined, would you please share a minute to review my book. Loved it, Hated it - I'd just enjoy your feedback.

As you May have gleaned from my books, reviews can be tough to come by these days and

You the reader have the power make or break the success of a book. If you'd be so kind to review the book, I would greatly appreciate it!

Thank you so much again for reading "**Psychology: Hypnosis & Mind Control – To Overcome Stress, Anxiety, Depression & Finally Recover Your Happiness**" and for spending time with me! I will see you in the next one!

Free Bonus!!!

We would like to Offer you Exclusive access to our Breakthrough Book Club!!! It's a place where

we offer a NEW FREE E-book every week! Also our members are actively discussing, reviewing, and sharing their thoughts on the Book of The Week and on topics to help each other Breakthrough Life's Obstacles! With a Chance to win a $25 Gift Card EVERY Month! Please Enjoy Your FREE Access here: https://www.facebook.com/groups/Breakthrough BookClub/

Check Out More From The Publisher…

Healthy Living: Mental Health, Find Happiness by Improving your Gut Health, Sugar Addiction, and IBS

by Maria Lexington

http://www.amazon.com/Healthy-Living-Happiness-Schizophrenia-Fibromyalgia-ebook/dp/B010KM9CLA

Marriage: Romance Your Mate Again, With Spicy Sex Secrets, Pleasure, Taboo And Sex Positions that will Blow Their Mind

by Veronica Counsel

http://www.amazon.com/Marriage-Pleasure-Positions-Intimacy-Counseling-ebook/dp/B016SGTEY2

Pregnancy: Baby Smart, What You Need to Know to Start a Family - Motherhood, Childbirth & Nutrition

by Kayla McCormick

http://www.amazon.com/Pregnancy-Childbirth-Motherhood-Everything-Breastfeeding-ebook/dp/B016ESNZSU

Social Media: Master Social Media Marketing - Facebook, Twitter, YouTube & Instagram

by Grant Kennedy

http://www.amazon.com/Social-Media-Marketing-Facebook-Instagram-ebook/dp/B018Y68SWS

Gardening: Hydroponics for Beginners: The Ultimate Guide to Hydroponic Gardening

by Melissa Honeydew

http://www.amazon.com/Hydroponics-Sufficiency-Vegetables-Homesteading-Preservation-ebook/dp/B01508IZAS

Fred McGuaghy

www.ingramcontent.com/pod-product-compliance
Lightning Source LLC
Chambersburg PA
CBHW072205280526
45788CB00002B/891